The Urbana Free Library

To renew: call 217-367-4057
or go to "*urbanafreelibrary.org*"
and select "Renew/Request Items"

ANIMAL ARMIES

LION PRIDES

RICHARD AND
LOUISE SPILSBURY

PowerKiDS press™
New York

Published in 2013 by The Rosen Publishing Group, Inc.
29 East 21st Street, New York, NY 10010

Copyright © 2013 by The Rosen Publishing Group, Inc.

Produced for Rosen by Calcium Creative Ltd
Editors for Calcium Creative Ltd: Sarah Eason and Katie Woolley
US Editor: Sara Antill
Designers: Paul Myerscough and Geoff Ward

Photo credits: Dreamstime: Smellme cover; Shutterstock: Aperture Untamed 8–9, Riaan van den Berg 20br, Dean Bertoncelj 6t, DarkOne 24r, Tilo G 22br, Pat Garvey 24–25, Jakub Gruchot 12r, JacoBecker 19t, Chris Kruger 18–19, Chad Littlejohn 20–21, Meunierd 28br, Stu Porter 26br, 28–29, Dave Pusey 14–15, J. Norman Reid 12–13, Uryadnikov Sergey 11b, Graeme Shannon 4–5, Jake Sorensen 16b, Nickolay Stanev 10–11, Villiers Steyn 22–23, Johan Swanepoel 26–27, Mogens Trolle 16–17, Gerrit de Vries 8b, Wild At Art 6–7, Peter Wollinga 1, 15r, Oleg Znamenskiy 4b.

Library of Congress Cataloging-in-Publication Data

Spilsbury, Richard, 1963–
 Lion prides / by Richard Spilsbury and Louise Spilsbury.
    p. cm. — (Animal armies)
 Includes index.
 ISBN 978-1-4777-0306-9 (library binding) — ISBN 978-1-4777-0334-2 (pbk.) —
ISBN 978-1-4777-0335-9 (6-pack)
 1. Lion—Behavior—Juvenile literature. 2. Social behavior in animals—Juvenile literature.
 3. Predatory animals—Juvenile literature. I. Spilsbury, Louise. II. Title.
 QL737.C23S587 2013
 599.757—dc23

                                      2012022324

Manufactured in the United States of America

CPSIA Compliance Information: Batch #W13PK2: For Further Information contact Rosen Publishing, New York, New York at 1-800-237-9932

CONTENTS

LIONS

Lions are big, powerful cats. Males can be around the same size as a small car and are very strong. Females are smaller, but are very powerful, too. Lions live in Africa where it is very hot and dry. They live in areas of savanna or scrub. These are places with wide open spaces, long grass, and few trees.

Although lions are often seen alone in the wild, they are **social** animals that live in groups. A group of lions is called a pride. There can be as few as three lions in a pride, or as many as 40 animals. Lions spend much of their time with other lions. They hunt for food, raise young, rest, and play with other members of their pride.

Lions in a pride care for each other. Being in the pride helps all of the group to survive.

Super Skills

A lion's long, brown fur helps it to blend in with the dry, brown grasses of its savanna **habitat**. The lion hides in the grass to sneak up on the animals it hunts.

Adult male lions have manes. This is a ring of long fur around the lion's head.

RANK

Different members of an army have different **ranks** and different jobs to do. This is also true of lion prides. Male and female lions have different ranks and jobs within the group. Most lion prides include just one or two adult males.

Male lions are of the highest rank in the pride and are in charge of the group. Their job is to **protect** the pride and **defend** its **territory**. Female lions are called lionesses. They do most of the hunting. Lionesses catch food for themselves and the other animals in the pride. They also look after the baby lions, which are called cubs. The lionesses in a pride are usually related. They are grandmothers, mothers, daughters, and sisters.

In a pride, adult males have a higher rank than adult females. Adult females have a higher rank than all of the cubs.

Males are the leaders of a pride. Even weak males have a higher rank than the females.

Who's Who?

Male lions have manes to make them look big and fierce. This helps to remind the females and cubs that the males are in charge.

ON PATROL

A pride's territory is the area in which the lions live, feed, and sleep. A pride chooses a territory in which there are lots of animals for them to hunt and water for them to drink. The male lions **patrol** the borders of the pride's territory. They guard it to stop other lions from getting in and taking their food.

To guard their territory, male lions walk around it and look out for **intruders**. They also mark the edges of the territory with scratches and smells. Males scratch the ground or trees to make marks. They spray strong-smelling **urine** onto bushes and tree trunks. These signs tell lions from other prides to keep out!

Lions choose a territory in which there is a watering hole, so the pride has enough to drink.

Young male lions help to patrol their pride's territory.

Who's Who?

Males roar loudly to say they are in charge and to warn other lions to stay away from their territory. These roars can be heard from as far away as 5 miles (8 km)!

HUNTING

Lions are carnivores, which means they eat the flesh of other animals. The lionesses in a pride usually hunt for food in the evenings. It is easier to catch animals when it is dark. Lionesses hunt in teams. By hunting together they can catch animals that are bigger than they are, such as zebras and **wildebeests**.

Lionesses often work in teams of two or three. Just like the soldiers in an army, these teams have **tactics**. Sometimes, the fitter, faster lionesses chase the **prey**. The stronger, heavier lionesses lie in wait, ready to pounce when the prey comes toward them. At other times, the whole team of lionesses forms a circle around a **herd** of animals. This stops the prey from escaping. The team of lionesses then close in on their trapped prey and kill it.

In areas of long grass, teams of lionesses may hunt during the day. The grass hides them from their prey as they sneak up on it.

Super Skills

Lions have special skills that help them to hunt in dim light. They can see almost as well at night as a human can in the day. Their ears can also hear prey from 1 mile (2 km) away!

Lions hunt and eat different animals. Their food includes small hares, **warthogs**, wildebeests, zebras, and buffalo.

13

FEEDING TIME

When a team of lionesses has caught and killed its prey, it's time for the pride to eat. Males eat first. They follow a hunting team, and run up as soon as dinner is served! They growl, hiss, and snap at the other lions to warn them to stand back.

Females have to wait until the males have finished before they can eat. They snarl while the males are eating. If the females did not do this, the males might go on feeding until there is nothing left! The cubs usually have to wait until last and eat what is left over. Some lion cubs even die before their first birthday because they do not get enough food to survive.

*Lions also eat dead animals that they find. They chase away **vultures** to eat the dead animal themselves.*

After the pride has eaten a large animal, lionesses may not need to hunt again for a few days.

Fight to Survive

Lions in a pride fight over prey because it may be several days until their next meal. Lionesses may only catch prey in one out of three (or more) hunting trips.

NEW RECRUITS

A lioness usually has three or four cubs at one time. When lion cubs are born, they are very small. They do not open their eyes until they are two weeks old, and cannot run until they are one month old. At first, cubs can't do anything for themselves. Mothers feed the cubs milk from their bodies and hide them somewhere safe, such as in a bush or among some rocks.

Many of the females in a pride have babies around the same time. They do this so they can care for, protect, and feed each other's young. Lionesses must hunt even while their babies are small. While some lionesses are hunting, the others in the pride act as babysitters. They watch over the new **recruits** to keep them safe. Lionesses can even feed milk to another lioness's baby.

Lionesses are very loving toward their cubs and very protective of them.

Lionesses in a pride help to look after each other's cubs.

Fight to Survive

Female lions have their cubs around the same time to give them a better chance of survival. Cubs in a pride are twice as likely to survive as cubs born to a lioness living on her own.

TRAINING

Lion cubs learn as they play. When they are very young, they often play with their mother's tail. She flicks her tail around and the cubs chase it and catch it. This helps them learn how to pounce on fast-moving prey. Young lion cubs also pounce on sticks and grab them with their sharp teeth. Then they shake their head from side to side, as they will do one day to kill their prey.

Once cubs can run, they follow and watch their mother hunting. They watch how she sneaks up on prey and how she works with other lionesses to catch it. The cubs then practice these moves themselves, sometimes by chasing and pouncing on each other! Young lions can start hunting at around two years old.

Cubs learn useful skills when they play fight together.

Super Skills

Cubs must learn to hunt to survive. A lioness sometimes brings live-but-injured prey back to her cubs. Then the cubs can practice catching and killing the prey for themselves.

Cubs follow their mother on hunting trips to watch and learn from her.

TALKING

Teams must be able to talk to each other to work together. Lions in a pride pass on messages using sounds and signals. Lions make different sounds to say different things.

Mothers make low, grunting sounds to call to babies. Cubs make small, mewing sounds to greet their mother. Lionesses call to each other when they are hunting in the dark. Lions use **body language** to talk, too. They bare their teeth to show anger. They flick their tail and bend their head low to show they are about to attack. Young lions open their mouths, but keep their teeth covered to show other lions that they want to play!

Male lions usually roar loudly to warn off intruders in the early evening.

One lion may bow its head slightly to another. This shows that it knows the lion is of a higher rank.

Who's Who?

There are sometimes fights between lions from the same pride. To stop the fight, the weaker lion lies on its back. This tells the stronger lion that the other lion knows he is the boss!

OFF DUTY

Lions are off duty most of the time! It can be very hot in the parts of Africa where they live. To keep cool, lions mostly hunt or patrol their territory during the late afternoon or evening, when it is cooler. They spend most of the day lying around and sleeping. This helps to keep them cool in the hot sunshine.

Lions usually rest under the shade of a tree or in the grass. Lions can climb well, so they stretch out on tree branches, too. When they are sleeping or relaxing, the lions in a pride often lie close together. They sleep with their legs and tails draped over each other. Lion cubs rest hidden in long, dry grass where they are safe from the **predators** that hunt them.

Cubs are the same color as grass. This helps them to hide.

Lions often lie together when they sleep or relax. They rub each other's heads and purr to show they are happy.

Fight to Survive

Lions may look lazy, but it is important that they rest. Males sleep for 20 hours a day to build up energy. They are then ready to leap up for a chase or a dangerous fight!

TEAM BUILDING

While lions rest and relax, they often **groom** each other. Grooming keeps an animal's fur clean and removes insects that can spread disease. It also helps to make all of the pride feel that they are part of a team.

Lions have a special way of greeting the other members of their pride. When they meet a lion of the same pride, they rub cheeks with it. Sometimes they rub their necks and bodies together, too. These actions are a little like a handshake or a hug. The greetings remind the lions in a pride that they are friends and are all part of the same group.

Cubs must learn to greet other members of their pride, too!

Lionesses do most of the grooming in a pride. They groom the cubs and the males as well as each other.

Super Skills

Lions have a hard and bumpy tongue. This helps them to groom. The bumps on the tongue help to remove blood from fur after feeding. The bumps also remove fleas and other insects.

CHANGES IN THE PRIDE

Female cubs stay with their mother's pride their entire lives. Males leave the group when they are around three years old. Sometimes they choose to leave. Other times the older males in the pride chase them away. Young male lions that have been forced to leave a pride join together in small gangs. They travel and hunt together, sometimes following large herds of prey.

When a young male lion has grown big and strong, he tries to join or take over a new pride. To do this, he must fight the males already in the pride. If the leaders of a pride are old and weak, he might be able to kill them or chase them away. He can then take over the pride and its territory.

A male's mane becomes darker as he grows older.

Young male lions often roam together until they are five or six years old. Then they are strong enough to take over a pride of their own.

Fight to Survive

When a new male takes over a pride, he may kill all the cubs. He does this to make sure that he will be the father of all the cubs in the pride in the future.

DEFENDING THE PRIDE

Lions work as a team to protect other members of their pride. The lion cubs are the most **vulnerable**. **Hyenas**, leopards, **jackals**, and even crocodiles try to catch and eat cubs. If a cub is in danger, the other lions in the pride race to protect it. They surround the attacker and will fight and kill it if it doesn't run away.

Lions also protect injured lions in their pride. Adult lions can become injured while hunting strong prey. They can also be hurt when they fight lions from another pride. A pride will bring food to the injured lion and defend it against predators until it is well again. By caring for each other, lions make sure that the pride will survive.

Males are very protective of the cubs in their pride. They sometimes guard the cubs while the mother hunts.

Lions growl and show their long, sharp teeth as a warning. If this doesn't scare off an attacker, the lion will use its teeth to bite and kill.

Who's Who?

Male lions are the main defenders of the pride. They are very strong, heavy, and powerful. Their thick mane protects their throat when other animals fight them.

SURVIVAL

Prides also face danger from people. Some people kill lions to protect themselves or their animals. Others kill lions for sport. People also build homes and farms on land where lions live. This means that lions are forced to make smaller and smaller territories. Small territories have fewer animals for lions to hunt. This means that cubs may not get enough to eat and will die.

Some African countries are working to protect lions by creating **reserves** or national parks. These are areas of land where lions and their territories are protected. People cannot hunt, farm, or build in these areas. In protected places such as these, prides of lions can live and raise cubs safely. By creating more reserves, people can help lion prides to survive in the future.

When people build on land, there is less grass for zebras, buffalo, and other animals to eat. That means there are fewer animals for lions to hunt.

By living as a pride, lions have a better chance of survival in the wild.

Fight to Survive

Some people want lions to be listed as **endangered** animals. This would give lion prides extra protection and help to make sure they survive in the future.

GLOSSARY

body language (BAH-dee LANG-gwij) Actions animal use to talk.

defend (dih-FEND) To protect against attack.

endangered (in-DAYN-jerd) When an animal could die out.

groom (GROOM) To clean dirt, dead skin, or insects from fur.

habitat (HA-buh-tat) The place in which an animal hunts and lives.

herd (HURD) A group of plant-eating animals.

hyenas (hy-EE-nuhz) Wild dogs that live in Africa.

intruders (in-TROOD-erz) People or animals that are unwelcome.

jackals (JA-kulz) Wild dogs that live in Africa.

patrol (puh-TROHL) To move around an area to make sure it is safe.

predators (PREH-duh-terz) Animals that hunt other animals.

prey (PRAY) An animal that is eaten by other animals.

protect (pruh-TEKT) To keep safe.

ranks (RANKS) The positions within an army or a group.

recruits (rih-KROOTS) New members.

reserves (rih-ZURVZ) Areas of land where animals are protected.

social (SOH-shul) Friendly.

tactics (TAK-tiks) Tricks or ways of doing something.

territory (TER-uh-tor-ee) An area controlled by one animal group.

urine (YUR-un) A liquid waste made by the body.

vulnerable (VUL-neh-ruh-bel) Weak, open to attack.

vultures (VUHL-churz) Birds that feed on dead animals.

warthogs (WORT-hogz) Piglike creatures that live in Africa.

wildebeests (WIL-deh-beests) Large plant-eating creatures similar to buffalo.

FURTHER READING

Clark, Willow. *Lions: Life in the Pride*. Animal Families. New York: PowerKids Press, 2011.

Joubert, Dereck, and Beverly Joubert. *Face to Face with Lions*. Face to Face with Animals. Des Moines, IA: National Geographic Children's Books, 2010.

Owen, Ruth. *Lions*. Dr. Bob's Amazing World of Animals. New York: Windmill Books, 2012.

WEBSITES

Due to the changing nature of Internet links, PowerKids Press has developed an online list of websites related to the subject of this book. This site is updated regularly. Please use this link to access the list: **www.powerkidslinks.com/aarmy/lion/**

INDEX